Jesus
in the
Qur'an

Revised Edition

Ahmad Thomson and
Muhammad 'Ata'ur-Rahim

Ta-Ha Publishers Ltd.

© Ramadan 1433/August 2012 Ahmad Thomson

First Edition published by MWH London Publishers in 1979

Revised Edition published in 2012 by:
Ta-Ha Publishers Ltd.
Unit 4, The Windsor Centre
Windsor Grove, West Norwood
London SE27 9NT, United Kingdom

www.tahapublishers.com

Written by: Ahmad Thomson and Muhammad 'Ata'ur-Rahim
Revised and typeset by: Ahmad Thomson

A catalogue record of this book
is available from the British Library

ISBN   978-1-84200-131-8

Printed and bound by: IMAK Ofset, Turkey

Introduction

The first edition of *Jesus in the Qur'an* was simply Chapter Eleven of the first edition of *Jesus, Prophet of Islam* by Muhammad Ata'ur-Rahim, *alayhi rahma*, and Ahmad Thomson, first published by Diwan Press in 1977.

A revised and expanded edition of *Jesus, Prophet of Islam* was published by Ta-Ha Publishers Ltd in 1996. One of the features of this revised edition was that Chapter Eleven was expanded considerably.

This revised edition of *Jesus in the Qur'an* is simply Chapter Eleven of the revised and expanded edition of *Jesus, Prophet of Islam* by Muhammad Ata'ur-Rahim and Ahmad Thomson – but with one significant exception:

The translations into English of passages from the *Qur'an* in the first and revised editions of *Jesus, Prophet of Islam* were based on the translation of Muhammad Marmaduke Pickthall, *alayhi rahma*. In 1999, *The Noble Qur'an – a New Rendering of its Meaning in English* by Shaykh Abdalhaqq and Aisha Bewley was published by Bookwork, with revised editions being published in 2005 and 2011. With the generous permission of Shaykh Abdalhaqq and Aisha Bewley, their translation into English of the *Qur'an* has been used in this revised edition of *Jesus in the Qur'an*, as well as the definitions from their Glossaries of Terms and Proper Names which are to be found in the Glossary at the end of this book ~ thank you!

Ahmad Thomson
London, 2012

The likeness of Jesus in Allah's sight is the same as Adam. He created him from earth, and then He said to him: 'Be!' and he was.

It is the truth from your Lord
   so do not be among the doubters.

   (Qur'an: Surat Ali 'Imran – 3: 59-60)

Jesus in the Qur'an

The *Qur'an*, the last of the Divine Books, revealed by the Creator to the last of the Messengers – Muhammad, may God bless him and grant him peace – is a source of knowledge about Jesus, peace be upon him, which is not generally known to most students of Christianity. The *Qur'an* not only leads us towards a better understanding of who Jesus was, but also, through that understanding, it increases our respect and love for him. The last Revelation, coming as it did some six hundred years after the birth of Jesus, tells what is important for us to know about his life and teachings, and places his role as Prophet in the vast perspective that the Unitarians realised lay behind prophecy itself. The *Qur'an* alone gives us that perspective – which no other source today can provide.

The *Qur'an* does not cover the life of Jesus in any great detail as regards specific events. The miracles and powers which he was given are mentioned including some which are not even described in the Bible – but mostly in general terms. Similarly, the Book which Jesus was given by God, the *Injil*, is mentioned several times, but its exact contents are not indicated. However, the *Qur'an* is very specific as to his purpose, how he appeared on earth, who he was, and, equally important, who he was not, and how his mission ended.

Before looking at the verses which describe the life of Jesus himself, it would be helpful to examine the verses which delineate what his function on earth was, and how he fits into the broader pattern of what came before him and what was to come after him:

It is stated again and again that Jesus was one of the long line of Prophets who had been sent to the peoples of this earth; that he was a Messenger whose guidance and teachings were a reaffirmation and an extension of the guidance which the Prophets before him had brought – and a preparation for the guidance which the Prophet coming after him would bring, may God bless him and grant him peace.

The *Qur'an* makes it clear that Jesus was the son of Mary, the daughter of 'Imran, who was descended from the Prophet Solomon, the son of the Prophet David who was descended from Judah, one of the twelve sons of the Prophet Jacob – who was otherwise known as Israel – who was descended from the Prophet Isaac, the son of the Prophet Abraham, may the blessings and peace of God be on all of them.

The *Qur'an* also makes it clear that there is absolutely no doubt about the fact that Jesus was the promised Messiah – descended from the family of David, from the family of Jacob, from the family of the Prophet Abraham through his son Isaac – whose coming had been foretold in the original *Torah* of Moses, may the blessings and peace of God be on all of them:

> We gave Musa the Book
> and sent a succession of Messengers after him.
> We gave 'Isa, son of Maryam, the Clear Signs
> and reinforced him with the Purest Ruh.   (*Qur'an* 2: 87)

The following passage reminds us of the line of Prophets of which Jesus was a part. After referring to Abraham, it continues:

> We gave him Ishaq and Ya'qub,
>   each of whom We guided.
>   And before him We had guided Nuh.
> And among his descendants were Dawud and Sulayman,
>   and Ayyub, Yusuf, Musa and Harun.
> That is how We recompense the good-doers.
>
> And Zakariyya, Yahya, 'Isa and Ilyas.
>   All of them were among the righteous.
> And Isma'il, al-Yasa', Yunus and Lut.
>   All of them We favoured over all beings.
> And some of their forebears, descendants and brothers;
>   We chose them and guided them to a straight path.
>   (*Qur'an* 6: 84–87)

And this list of Prophets is by no means complete, as the following passage addressed to the Prophet Muhammad, makes clear:

> We have revealed to you as We revealed to Nuh
>   and the Prophets who came after him.
>   And We revealed to Ibrahim

and Isma'il and Ishaq and Ya'qub and the Tribes,
   and 'Isa and Ayyub and Yunus
   and Harun and Sulayman.
   And We gave Dawud the *Zabur*.

There are Messengers We have already told you about
   and Messengers We have not told you about;
   and Allah spoke directly to Musa –
Messengers bringing good news and giving warning,
   so that people will have no argument against Allah
   after the coming of the Messengers.
   Allah is Almighty, All-Wise.

(*Qur'an* 4: 163-165)

In fact the Prophet Muhammad said that Jesus was one of one hundred and twenty-four thousand Prophets, may the blessings and peace of God be on all of them, between whom there is no cause for conflict or argument. Thus God commands the Muslims as follows:

Say, 'We believe in Allah
   and what has been sent down to us
and what was sent down to Ibrahim, Isma'il and Ishaq
   and Ya'qub and the Tribes,
and what Musa and 'Isa and all the Prophets
   were given by their Lord.
We do not differentiate between any of them.
   We are Muslims submitted to Him.'

If anyone desires anything other than Islam as a deen,
   it will not be accepted from him,
and in the Next World he will be among the losers.

(*Qur'an* 3: 84-85)

Furthermore, it is clear from the *Qur'an* that all of the Prophets were well aware that they had been sent by God for the same purpose and with basically the same message:

When We made a covenant with all the Prophets –
   with you (Muhammad) and with Nuh and Ibrahim
   and Musa and 'Isa son of Maryam –

We made a binding covenant with them,
so that He might question the truly sincere
about their sincerity; and
He has prepared a painful punishment for the unbelievers.

(Qur'an 33: 7-8)

And:

Messengers, eat of the good things and act rightly.
I most certainly know what you do.

This faith of yours is a single faith
and I am your Lord,
so have taqwa of Me.   *(Qur'an* 23: 51-52)

And:

He has laid down the same deen for you
as He enjoined on Nuh:
that which We have revealed to you (Muhammad)
and which We enjoined on Ibrahim, Musa and 'Isa:
'Establish the deen and do not make divisions in it.'

(Qur'an 42: 13)

Part of the covenant which all the Prophets made with God was
to tell their followers about the coming of Muhammad, may God
bless him and grant him peace, and to follow him should he come
during their lifetime:

Remember when Allah made a covenant with the Prophets:
'Now that I have given you a share
of the Book and Wisdom,
and then a Messenger comes to you
confirming what is with you,
you must believe in him and help him.'
He asked, 'Do you agree and undertake My commission
on that condition?'
They replied, 'We agree.'
He said, 'Bear witness, then.
I am with you as one of the witnesses.'

Any who turn away after that
are deviators.   *(Qur'an* 3: 81-82)

Thus the picture of Jesus which unfolds in the *Qur'an* is not that of some remarkable man who appeared on earth as an isolated event in an otherwise somewhat chaotic world, but of a Messenger who, like all the other Messengers, was sent for his time and his age, a part of the ordered unfolding of the universe:

> And We sent 'Isa son of Maryam
>   following in their footsteps,
>   confirming the *Torah* that came before him.
> We gave him the *Injil* containing guidance and light
>   confirming the *Torah* that came before it, and
> as guidance and admonition for those who are godfearing.

> The people of the *Injil* should judge
>   by what Allah sent down in it.
> Those who do not judge by what Allah has set down,
>   such people are deviators.
>
> *(Qur'an* 5: 46-47)

And furthermore, a time which, as Jesus was well aware, had limits – a time which was bounded by the time before his time, and by the time after it:

> Remember when Musa said to his people,
>   'My people, why do you mistreat me
> when you know that I am the Messenger of Allah to you?'
>   So when they deviated,
>   Allah made their hearts deviate.
> Allah does not guide people who are deviators.

> And when 'Isa son of Maryam said,
>   'Tribe of Israel, I am the Messenger of Allah to you,
>   confirming the *Torah* which came before me
>   and giving you the good news of a Messenger after me
>   whose name is Ahmad.'

('*Ahmad* is one of the names of the Prophet Muhammad, may God bless him and grant him peace, meaning 'the Most Praiseworthy', 'the One who Distinguishes between Truth and Falsehood', and 'the Comforter'. Its equivalent in Greek is '*Parakletos*' or '*Parakleitos*', meaning 'the Comforter' or 'the Praised One'.)

When he brought them the Clear Signs,
  they said, 'This is downright magic.'

Who could do greater wrong than someone
  who invents a lie against Allah
    when he has been called to Islam?
  Allah does not guide wrongdoing people.

They desire to extinguish Allah's Light
  with their mouths
but Allah will perfect His Light,
  though the unbelievers hate it.

It is He who sent His Messenger with guidance
  and the Deen of Truth
to exalt it over every other deen,
  though the idolators hate it.

You who believe! shall I direct you to a transaction
  which will save you from a painful punishment?
It is to believe in Allah and His Messenger
  and do jihad in the Way of Allah
    with your wealth and your selves.
  That is better for you if you only knew.

He will forgive you your wrong actions
  and admit you into Gardens
    with rivers flowing under them,
and fine dwellings in the Gardens of Eden.
  That is the Great Victory.
  And other things you love:
support from Allah and imminent victory.
  Give good news to the believers!

You who believe! be helpers of Allah
  as 'Isa son of Maryam said to the Disciples,
    'Who will be my helpers to Allah?'
The Disciples said, 'We will be the helpers of Allah.'
  One faction of the tribe of Israel believed
    and the other disbelieved.

So We supported those who believed against their enemy
and they became victorious.

(*Qur'an* 61: 5-14)

Jesus's conception and birth are recorded by the *Qur'an* in great
detail. It would be illuminating to begin with his mother's birth
and upbringing, for it helps us to see how Mary was chosen and
prepared by God to be the mother of Jesus:

Allah chose Adam and Nuh
and the family of Ibrahim
and the family of 'Imran
over all other beings –
descendants one of the other.
Allah is All-Hearing, All-Knowing.

Remember when the wife of 'Imran said,
'My Lord, I have pledged to You
what is in my womb,
devoting it to Your service.
Please accept my prayer.
You are the All-Hearing, the All-Knowing.'

When she gave birth, she said,
'My Lord! I have given birth to a girl' –
and Allah knew very well what she had given birth to,
male and female are not the same –
'and I have named her Maryam
and placed her and her children
in Your safekeeping from the accursed Shaytan.'

Her Lord accepted her with approval
and made her grow in health and beauty.
And Zakariyya became her guardian.
Every time Zakariyya visited her in the Upper Room,
he found food with her.
He said, 'Maryam, how did you come by this?'
She said, 'It is from Allah.
Allah provides for whomever He wills
without any reckoning.'

Then and there Zakariyya called on his Lord and said,
'O Lord, grant me by Your favour an upright child.
You are the Hearer of Prayer.'

The angels called out to him
while he was standing in prayer in the Upper Room:
'Allah gives you the good news of Yahya,
who will come to confirm a Word (Jesus) from Allah,
and will be a leader and a celibate,
a Prophet and one of the righteous.'

He said, 'My Lord, how can I possibly have a son
when I have reached old age and my wife is barren?'
He said, 'It will be so.
Allah does whatever He wills.'

He said, 'My Lord, appoint a Sign for me.'
He said, 'Your Sign is that you will not speak
to people for three days,
except by gesture.
Remember your Lord much and glorify Him
in the evening and after dawn.'

And when the angels said, 'Maryam, Allah has chosen you
and purified you.
He has chosen you over all other women.
Maryam, obey your Lord and prostrate
and bow with those who bow.'

This is news from the Unseen which We reveal to you.
You were not with them when they cast their reeds
to see which of them would be the guardian of Maryam.
You were not with them when they quarrelled.

(Qur'an 3: 33–44)

John was the Prophet who directly preceded Jesus. It is said that his mother, Elisabeth, and Mary's mother, Hannah, were either sisters or cousins, which means that Jesus and John were cousins. The miraculous birth of John is also mentioned in the following passages:

And Zakariyya when he called out to his Lord,

'My Lord, do not leave me on my own,
  though You are the Best of Inheritors.'
We responded to him and gave him Yahya,
  restoring for him his wife's fertility.
They outdid each other in good actions,
  calling out to Us in yearning and in awe,
    and humbling themselves to Us.

And she who protected her private parts (Mary).
  We breathed into her some of Our Ruh
and made her and her son (Jesus) a Sign for all the worlds.

(*Qur'an* 21: 89-91)

And:

Remembering your Lord's mercy to His slave Zakariyya,
  when he called on his Lord in secret
    and said, 'My Lord,
  my bones have lost their strength
    and my head is crowned with white,
  but in calling on You, my Lord,
    I have never been disappointed.
  I fear my relatives when I am gone
    and my wife is barren,
  so give me an heir from You
    to be my inheritor
  and the inheritor of the family of Ya'qub,
    and make him, my Lord, pleasing to You.'

'Zakariyya! We give you the good news
  of a boy named Yahya,
a name We have given to no one else before.'

He said, 'My Lord! How can I have a boy
  when my wife is barren
and I have reached advanced old age?'

He said, 'It will be so!
  Your Lord says, "That is easy for Me to do.
I created you before, when you were not anything."'

He said, 'My Lord, give me a Sign.'
  He said, 'Your Sign is not to speak to people
    for three nights
    despite the fact that you are perfectly able to.'

He came out to his people from the Upper Room
  and gestured to them to glorify Allah
    in the morning and the evening.

'Yahya, take hold of the Book with vigour.'
  We gave him judgement while still a child,
    and tenderness and purity from Us –
      he was godfearing –
    and devotion to his parents –
he was not insolent or disobedient.

Peace be upon him the day he was born,
  and the day he dies,
and the day he is raised up again alive.   (*Qur'an* 19: 2-15)

The story of the miraculous conception and birth of Jesus is related in two different places in the *Qur'an*:

When the angels said, 'Maryam, Allah
  gives you good news of a Word from Him.
His name is the Messiah, 'Isa, son of Maryam,
  of high esteem in this world and the Next World,
    and one of those brought near.
He will speak to people in the cradle,
  and also when fully grown,
    and will be one of the righteous,'
she said, 'My Lord! How can I have a son
  when no man has ever touched me?'
He said, 'It will be so.'
  Allah creates whatever He wills.
When He decides on something,
  He just says to it, 'Be!' and it is.
He will teach him the Book and Wisdom,
  and the *Torah* and the *Injil,*
as a Messenger to the tribe of Israel, saying:

'I have brought you a Sign from your Lord.
I will create the shape of a bird out of clay for you
    and then breathe into it and it will be a bird
        by Allah's permission.
I will heal the blind and lepers,
    and bring the dead to life,
        by Allah's permission.
I will tell you what you eat
    and what you store up in your homes.
    There is a Sign for you in that if you are believers.
I come confirming the *Torah* I find already there,
    and to make lawful for you
    some of what was previously forbidden to you.
I have brought you a Sign from your Lord.
    So have taqwa of Allah and obey me.
Allah is my Lord and your Lord so worship Him.
    That is a straight path.'

When 'Isa sensed unbelief on their part,
    he said, 'Who will be my helpers to Allah?'
The disciples said, 'We are Allah's helpers.
    We believe in Allah.
    Bear witness that we are Muslims.
Our Lord, we believe in what You have sent down
    and have followed the Messenger,
so write us down among the witnesses.'   (*Qur'an* 3: 45-53)

The story is also told in Surah Maryam:

Mention Maryam in the Book,
    how she withdrew from her people
        to an eastern place,
    and veiled herself from them.
Then We sent Our Ruh to her
    and it took on for her the form
        of a handsome, well-built man.
She said, 'I seek refuge from you with the All-Merciful
    if you are godfearing.'

He said, 'I am only your Lord's messenger
   so that He may give you a pure boy.'
She said, 'How can I have a boy
      when no man has touched me
      and I am not an unchaste woman?'
He said, 'It will be so!
      Your Lord says, "That is easy for Me.
It is so that We can make him a Sign for mankind
      and a mercy from Us."
It is a matter already decreed.'

So she conceived him and withdrew with him
      to a distant place.
The pains of labour drove her to the trunk of a date-palm.
   She said, 'Oh if only I had died before this time
      and were something discarded and forgotten!'

A voice called out to her from under her,
      'Do not grieve! Your Lord has placed
      a small stream at your feet.
   Shake the trunk of the palm towards you
      and fresh, ripe dates will drop down onto you.
   Eat and drink and delight your eyes.
      If you should see anyone at all, just say,
      "I have made a vow of silence to the All-Merciful
      and today I will not speak to any human being."'

She brought him to her people, carrying him.
   They said, 'Maryam! You have done
      an unthinkable thing!
Sister of Harun, your father was not an evil man
      nor was your mother an unchaste woman!'
She pointed towards him.
   They said, 'How can a baby in the cradle speak?'
He said, 'I am the slave of Allah,
      He has given me the Book and made me a Prophet.
      He has made me blessed wherever I am
   and directed me to pray and pay zakat
         as long as I live,
      and to show devotion to my mother.

He has not made me insolent or arrogant.
   Peace be upon me the day I was born,
      and the day I die
     and the day I am raised up again alive.'

That is 'Isa, son of Maryam,
   the word of truth
about which they are in doubt.

It is not fitting for Allah to have a son.
   Glory be to Him!
When He decides on something,
   He just says to it, 'Be!' and it is.

'Allah is my Lord and your Lord
   so worship Him.
This is a straight path.'   (*Qur'an* 19: 16-36)

The place where Jesus was born is also mentioned in one other passage in the *Qur'an*:

And We made the son of Maryam and his mother a Sign
   and gave them shelter on a mountainside
where there was a meadow and a flowing spring.

      (*Qur'an* 23: 50)

It is also said that this passage refers to the place where Mary and Jesus took refuge after his birth, and after they had been forced to leave Jerusalem and flee to Egypt, where they stayed during the early part of Jesus's childhood. God knows best.

    Jesus's childhood, his return to Jerusalem from Egypt with his mother, and his early manhood, are not mentioned in the *Qur'an*, but there are several references to what happened once he began to call the Tribe of Israel to only worship God and to follow the teachings of Moses which were in the *Torah*. The following passage, for example, refers to the response of the men who became Jesus's disciples:

You who believe! be helpers of Allah,
   as 'Isa son of Maryam said to the Disciples,
     'Who will be my helpers to Allah?'
The Disciples said, 'We will be the helpers of Allah.'

> One faction of the tribe of Israel believed
>   and the other disbelieved.
> So We supported those who believed against their enemy
>   and they became victorious.
>
> (*Qur'an* 61: 14)

The conflict between those who accepted Jesus and those who rejected him, peace be on him, often focused around his extraordinary
miracles, which he always attributed to God and not to himself. It
is not surprising, in view of these miracles, that some of those who
accepted Jesus did so rather too enthusiastically, and in so doing
mistakenly considered him to be the 'son' of God, thereby idolising
him and making him an object of worship. God refers to this mis-
conception in the following passage from *Surat al-Ma'ida*, which
refers to God's questioning all His Messengers on the Last Day:

> On the Day Allah gathers the Messengers together
>   and says, 'What response did you receive?'
> they will say, 'We do not know.
>   You are the Knower of unseen things.'

> Remember when Allah will say, "Isa, son of Maryam,
>   remember My blessing to you and to your mother
> when I reinforced you with the Purest Ruh
>   so that you could speak to people in the cradle
>   and when you were fully grown;
> and when I taught you the Book and Wisdom,
>   and the *Torah* and the *Injil*;
> and when you created a bird-shape out of clay
>   by My permission,
> and then breathed into it and it became a bird
>   by My permission;
> and healed the blind and the leper
>   by My permission;
> and when you brought forth the dead
>   by My permission;
> and when I held back the tribe of Israel from you,
>   when you brought them the Clear Signs
> and those of them who disbelieved said,
>   "This is nothing but downright magic";

and when I inspired the Disciples to believe
 in Me and in My Messenger,
they said, "We believe,
 Bear witness that we are Muslims.'''

And when the Disciples said, "Isa son of Maryam!
 Can your Lord send down a table to us out of heaven?'
He said, 'Have tawqa of Allah if you are believers!'

They said, 'We want to eat from it
 and for our hearts to be at peace
and to know that you have told us the truth
 and to be among those who witness it.'

'Isa son of Maryam said, 'Allah, our Lord,
 send down a table to us out of heaven
  to be a feast for us,
   for the first and last of us,
  and as a Sign from You.
 Provide for us!
  You are the Best of Providers!'

Allah said, 'I will send it down to you
 but if anyone among you disbelieves after that,
I will punish him with a punishment the like of which
 I will not inflict on anyone else in all the worlds!'

(It is said that this feast replenished itself as long as no
one stored up any of it for the next day, and that as soon
as someone did this, it disappeared. God knows best.)

And when Allah says, "Isa son of Maryam!
 Did you say to people, "Take me and my mother
  as gods besides Allah?"'
he will say, 'Glory be to You!
 It is not for me to say what I have no right to say!
If I had said it, then You would have known it.
 You know what is in my self
  but I do not know what is in Your Self.
 You are the Knower of all unseen things.
I said to them nothing but what You ordered me to say:
 "Worship Allah, my Lord and your Lord."

I was a witness against them
    as long as I remained among them,
but when You took me back to You,
    You were the One watching over them.
        You are Witness of all things.
    If You punish them,
        they are Your slaves.
    If You forgive them,
You are the Almighty, the All-Wise.'

Allah will say, 'This is the Day
    when the sincerity of the sincere
    will benefit them.
They will have Gardens
    with rivers flowing under them,
remaining in them timelessly,
    for ever and ever.
Allah is pleased with them
    and they are pleased with Him.
That is the Great Victory.'

The kingdom of the heavens and the earth
    and everything in them
        belongs to Allah.
    He has power over all things.   (*Qur'an* 5: 109-120)

Elsewhere in the *Qur'an*, God makes it perfectly clear that both Jesus and Mary were only human beings:

The Messiah, the son of Maryam, was only a Messenger,
    before whom other Messengers came and went.
His mother was a woman of truth.
    Both of them ate food.
See how We make the Signs clear to them!
    Then see how they are perverted!

Say: 'Do you worship, besides Allah,
    something which has no power to harm or help you
        when Allah is the All-Hearing, the All-Knowing?'

(*Qur'an* 5: 75-76)

It follows that Jesus could not possibly be the 'son' of God:

> They say, 'Allah has a son.'
>   Glory be to Him!
> No, everything in the heavens and earth belongs to Him.
>   Everything is obedient to Him,
> the Originator of the heavens and earth.
>   When He decides on something,
> He just says to it, 'Be!' and it is.   (*Qur'an* 2: 116-117)

And:

> Allah has no son
>   and there is no other god accompanying Him,
> for then each god would have gone off with what he created
>   and one of them would have been exalted
>   above the other.
>   Glory be to Allah above what they describe,
>   Knower of the Unseen and the Visible!
> May He be exalted above all they associate with Him!
>   (*Qur'an* 23: 91-92)

And:

> Indeed is the sincere deen not Allah's alone?
>   If people take protectors besides Him –
> 'We only worship them so that they
>   may bring us nearer to Allah' –
> Allah will judge between them regarding
>   the things about which they differed.
> Allah does not guide anyone who is an ungrateful liar.
>
> If Allah had desired to have a son
>   He would have chosen
>   whatever He wished
>   from what He has created.
>   Glory be to Him!
> He is Allah, the One, the All-Conquering! (*Qur'an* 39: 3-4)

And:

> Say: 'If the All-Merciful had a son,
>   I would be the first to worship him.'

> Glory be to the Lord of the heavens and the earth,
>> the Lord of the Throne,
>>> beyond what they describe.   (*Qur'an* 43: 81-82)

And:

> If you ask them, 'Who created the heavens and the earth?'
> they will say, 'Allah.'
> Say: 'So what do you think?
>> If Allah desires harm for me,
> can those you call upon besides Allah remove His harm?
>> Or if He desires mercy for me,
> can they withhold His mercy?'
>> Say: 'Allah is enough for me.
> All those who truly trust put their trust in Him.'

>>>> (*Qur'an* 39: 38)

And:

> Say: 'Do you order me to worship
>> something other than Allah,
>>> you ignorant people?'   (*Qur'an* 39: 64)

And:

> Blessed be He who has sent down the Furqan to His slave,
>> so that he can be a warner to all beings;
>>> He to whom the kingdom
>> of the heavens and the earth belongs.
>>> He does not have a son
>> and He has no partner in the Kingdom.
> He created everything and determined it most exactly.

> But they have adopted gods apart from Him
>> which do not create anything
>>> but are themselves created.
>> They have no power to harm or help themselves.
> They have no power over death or life or resurrection.

>>>> (*Qur'an* 25: 1-3)

And:

> They say, 'The All-Merciful has a son.'
>> They have devised a monstrous thing.

The heavens are all but rent apart
  and the earth split open
and the mountains brought crashing down,
    at their ascription of a son to the All-Merciful!
It is not fitting for the All-Merciful to have a son.

There is no one in the heavens and earth
    who will not come to the All-Merciful as a slave.
He has counted them and numbered them precisely.
    Each of them will come to Him on the Day of Rising
      all alone.

(Qur'an 19: 88-95)

And:

We sent no Messenger before you
    without revealing to him:
'There is no god but Me, so worship Me.'

They say, 'The All-Merciful has a son.'
    Glory be to Him!
No, they are honoured slaves!
    They do not precede Him in speech
      and they act on His command.

He knows what is in front of them and what is behind them.
    They only intercede on behalf of those
      with whom He is pleased,
    and even they are apprehensive out of fear of Him.
Were any of them to say,
    'I am a god apart from Him,'
We would repay him with Hell.
    That is how We repay wrongdoers.   (*Qur'an* 21: 25-29)

And:

They say: 'Allah has a son.'
    Glory be to Him!
He is the Rich Beyond Need.
    Everything in the heavens
      and everything on the earth
        belongs to Him.

> Have you authority to say this
>   or are you saying about Allah
>   what you do not know?
>
> Say: 'People who invent lies against Allah
>   will not be successful.'
> There is the enjoyment of this world.
>   Then they will return to Us.
> Then We will let them taste
>   the terrible punishment
>   because they disbelieved.   (*Qur'an* 10: 68-70)

Thus in the opening *ayat* of *Surat al-Kahf,* God states that one of the reasons why the *Qur'an* has been revealed is to warn those who claim that God has a son:

> In the name of Allah, All-Merciful, Most Merciful
>
> Praise belongs to Allah
>   Who has sent down the Book to His slave
>   and has put no crookedness in it.
> It is straight, to warn of violent force direct from Him,
>   and to give the good news to the believers,
>   those who do right actions,
>   that for them there is an excellent reward,
>   a place in which they will remain for ever,
>   and to warn those who say, 'Allah has a son.'
> They have no knowledge of this,
>   neither they nor their fathers.
> It is a monstrous utterance
>   which has issued from their mouths.
> What they say is nothing but a lie.   (*Qur'an* 18: 1-5)

For:

> It is not fitting for Allah to have a son.
>   Glory be to Him!
> When He decides on something,
>   He just says to it, 'Be!' and it is.   (*Qur'an* 19: 35)

And:

Mankind! an example has been made,
  so listen to it carefully.
Those whom you call upon besides Allah
  are not even able to create a single fly,
    even if they were to join together to do it.
  And if a fly steals something from them,
    they cannot get it back.
How feeble are both the seeker and the sought!

                                      (*Qur'an* 22: 73)

Thus it also follows that anyone who thinks – by virtue of Mary's degree of perfection, and by virtue of the miraculous nature of the immaculate conception – that Jesus can somehow be associated with being God in any way is mistaken:

Those who say, 'Allah is the Messiah, son of Maryam,'
  disbelieve.
Say: 'Who possesses any power at all over Allah
  if He desires to destroy the Messiah, son of Maryam,
    and his mother, and everyone else on earth?'
The kingdom of the heavens and the earth
  and everything between them
    belongs to Allah.
  He creates whatever He wills.
Allah has power over all things.   (*Qur'an* 5: 17)

It also follows that any concept of a Trinity is false:

People of the Book! do not go to excess in your deen.
  Say nothing but the truth about Allah.
The Messiah, 'Isa son of Maryam,
  was only the Messenger of Allah
    and His Word, which He cast into Maryam,
    and a Spirit from Him.
So believe in Allah and His Messengers.
  Do not say, 'Three.'
    It is better that you stop.
Allah is only One God!
  He is too Glorious to have a son!

Everything in the heavens and in the earth belongs to Him.
Allah suffices as a Guardian.

The Messiah would never disdain to be a slave to Allah
nor would the angels near to Him.
If any do disdain to worship Him, and grow arrogant,
He will in any case gather them all to Him.
As for those who believe and do right actions,
He will pay them their wages in full
and will give them increase from His favour.
As for those who show disdain and grow arrogant,
He will punish them with a painful punishment.
They will not find any protector or helper for themselves
besides Allah.

(Qur'an 4: 171-173)

And:

Those who say that the Messiah, son of Maryam, is Allah
are unbelievers.
The Messiah said: 'Tribe of Israel! worship Allah,
my Lord and your Lord.
If anyone associates anything with Allah,
Allah has forbidden him the Garden
and his refuge will be the Fire.'
The wrongdoers will have no helpers.

Those who say that Allah is the third of three
are unbelievers.
There is no god but One God.
If they do not stop saying what they say,
a painful punishment will afflict
those among them who disbelieve.

Why do they not turn to Allah and ask for His forgiveness?
Allah is Ever-Forgiving, Most Merciful.

(Qur'an 5: 72-74)

Jesus is also referred to in this passage from *Surat al-Baqara*, in
which God indicates that although some of His Messengers were
more blessed than others, this does not mean that they were not
human beings:

These Messengers: We favoured some of them over others.
    Allah spoke directly to some of them
        and raised up some of them in rank.
We gave Clear Signs to 'Isa, son of Maryam,
    and reinforced him with the Purest Ruh.
If Allah had willed, those who came after them
    would not have fought each other
        after the Clear Signs came to them,
            but they differed.
Among them there are those who believe
    and among them there are those who disbelieve.
If Allah had willed, they would not have fought each other.
But Allah does whatever He desires.

(*Qur'an* 2: 253)

Thus in spite of his extraordinary purity, and the piercing clarity of his words and signs, there were inevitably people who rejected Jesus, both while he was on earth and after he had been taken away from it:

When an example is made of the son of Maryam
    your people laugh uproariously.
They retort, 'Who is better then, our gods or him?'
    They only say this to you for argument's sake.
        They are indeed a disputatious people.
He is only a slave on whom We bestowed Our blessing
    and whom We made an example for the tribe of Israel.

If We wished We could appoint angels in exchange for you
    to succeed you on the earth.

He is a Sign of the Hour.
    Have no doubt about it.
But follow me.
    This is a straight path
Do not let Shaytan bar your way.
    He truly is an outright enemy to you.

And when 'Isa came with the Clear Signs,
    he said, 'I have come to you with Wisdom

and to clarify for you some of the things
    about which you have differed.
Therefore have taqwa of Allah and obey me.
    Allah is my Lord and your Lord
        so worship Him.
    This is a straight path.'

The various factions among them differed.
    Woe then to those who did wrong
on account of the punishment of a painful Day!

(Qur'an 43: 57-65)

And:

We sent Nuh and Ibrahim
    and placed Prophethood and the Book
        among their descendants.
Some of them are guided but many of them are deviators.

Then We sent Our Messengers following in their footsteps
    and sent 'Isa son of Maryam after them,
        giving him the *Injil.*
We put compassion and mercy
    in the hearts of those who followed him.
They invented monasticism –
    We did not prescribe it for them –
purely out of desire to gain the pleasure of Allah,
    but even so they did not observe it
    as it should have been observed.
To those of them who believed We gave their reward
    but many of them are deviators.

(Qur'an 57: 26-27)

Although both the Romans and the Pharisees wanted Jesus dead,
albeit for different reasons, God makes it clear that they did not kill
Jesus, even though it was their intention to do so:

They plotted and Allah plotted.
    But Allah is the best of plotters.

When Allah said, "Isa, I will take you back
    and raise you up to Me
and purify you of those who disbelieve.

And I will place the people who follow you
    above those who disbelieve until the Day of Rising.
Then you will all return to Me,
    and I will judge between you
regarding the things about which you differed.
    As for those who disbelieve,
I will punish them with a harsh punishment
    in this world and the Next World.
      They will have no helpers.'

As for those who believe and do right actions,
    We will pay them their wages in full.
      Allah does not love wrongdoers.

That is what We recite to you
    of the Signs and the wise Reminder.

The likeness of 'Isa in Allah's sight is the same as Adam.
    He created him from earth
and then He said to him, 'Be!' and he was.

It is the truth from your Lord
    so do not be among the doubters.

If anyone argues with you about him
    after the knowledge that has come to you,
say, 'Come then! Let us summon our sons and your sons,
    our women and your women,
      ourselves and yourselves.
    Then let us make earnest supplication
and call down the curse of Allah upon the liars.'

This is the true account:
    there is no other god besides Allah.
Allah – He is the Almighty, the All-Wise.

And if they turn away,
    Allah knows the corrupters.   (*Qur'an* 3: 54-63)

God also refers to the fact that Jesus was neither killed nor crucified
in the following passage from *Surat an-Nisa*, in which He describes
the consequences of the actions of those from among the Tribe of
Israel who disbelieved and broke their covenant with God:

Because of the fact that they broke their covenant,
   and rejected Allah's Signs,
and killed the Prophets without any right to do so
   and said, 'Our hearts are uncircumcised,'
Allah has stamped them with unbelief,
   so they do not believe except for very few.

And on account of their unbelief,
   and their utterance of a monstrous slander
      against Maryam,
and their saying, 'We killed the Messiah,
   'Isa son of Maryam, Messenger of Allah.'
They did not kill him and they did not crucify him
   but it was made to seem so to them.
Those who argue about him are in doubt about it.
   They have no real knowledge of it, just conjecture.
   But they certainly did not kill him.
   Allah raised him up to Himself.
   Allah is Almighty, All-Wise.
There is not one of the People of the Book
   who will not believe in him before he dies;
      and on the Day of Rising
      he will be a witness against them.

Because of the wrongdoing on the part of the Jews,
   We made unlawful for them some good things
      which had previously been lawful for them;
and because of their obstructing many people
   from the Way of Allah,
and because of their practising riba
   when they were forbidden to do it,
and because of their consuming people's wealth
   by wrongful means,
We have prepared for the unbelievers among them
   a painful punishment.

But those of them who are firmly rooted in knowledge,
   and the believers,
believe in what has been sent down to you
   and what was sent down before you:

those who establish the prayer and pay zakat,
    and believe in Allah and the Last Day –
We will pay such people an immense wage.

(*Qur'an* 4: 155-162)

The *Qur'an* makes it clear that the last Messenger to be sent by
God, not only to the Tribe of Israel, but to all mankind, and to the
jinn, was the Prophet Muhammad, may God bless him and grant
him peace, who confirmed the teachings of both Moses and Jesus,
while at the same time simplifying and abrogating their Law:

Allah made a covenant with the tribe of Israel
    and We raised up twelve leaders from among them.
Allah said, 'I am with you.
    If you establish the prayer and pay zakat,
        and believe in My Messengers
            and respect and support them,
        and make a generous loan to Allah,
    I will erase your wrong actions from you
        and admit you into Gardens
            with rivers flowing under them.
    Any of you who disbelieve after that
        have gone astray from the right way.'

But because of their breaking of their covenant,
    We have cursed them and made their hearts hard.
They distort the true meaning of words
    and have forgotten a good portion
        of what they were reminded of.
You will never cease to come upon
    some act of treachery on their part,
        except for a few of them.
Yet pardon them, and overlook.
    Allah loves good-doers.

We also made a covenant with those who say,
    'We are Christians,'
and they too forgot a good portion
    of what they were reminded of.

So We stirred up enmity and hatred between them
    until the Day of Rising
when Allah will inform them about what they did.

People of the Book! Our Messenger has come to you,
    making clear to you much of the Book
        that you have kept concealed,
            and passing over a lot.
    A Light has come to you from Allah
    and a Clear Book.

By it, Allah guides
    those who follow what pleases Him
        to the ways of Peace.
He will bring them from the darkness to the light
    by His permission,
and guide them to a straight path.   (*Qur'an* 5: 12-16)

As the above passage indicates, it was inevitable that when the
Prophet Muhammad, may God bless him and grant him peace,
began to call people to only worship God, many of them would
be those who claimed to be following either Moses or Jesus, and
it is for this reason that there are so many passages in the *Qur'an*
which are addressed to such people, who are often referred to as
the 'People of the Book' a title indicating – more then than now –
both their common genealogical link with the Tribe of Israel as
well as the fact that their way of life was, and is, at least to some
extent still based on one of the earlier divine revelations.

Although many of these passages may appear to have been
directed primarily towards the followers of Middle Eastern and
North African Judaism and Christianity who were alive when the
Qur'an was first revealed during the early seventh century AD, it is
clear that they often apply equally, if not more so, to the followers of
the various European versions of Judaism and Christianity which, as
we have already seen, developed at a later stage. It is equally clear that
they still often apply towards today's Jews and Christians, whatever
the version of Judaism or Christianity that they may now claim to
be following. In the *Qur'an* God promises those from among the
People of the Book who are sincere in their actions that they will
have nothing to fear:

Those who believe and those who are Jews
    and the Sabaeans and the Christians,
all who believe in Allah and the Last Day and act rightly
    will feel no fear and will know no sorrow.

                                               (Qur'an 5: 69)

And that they will receive what is due to them:

Those who believe, those who are Jews,
    and the Christians and Sabaeans,
all who believe in Allah and the Last Day and act rightly,
    will have their reward with their Lord.
They will feel no fear and and will know no sorrow.

                                             (Qur'an 2: 62)

And that God will judge between them on the Last Day:

As for those who believe
    and those who are Jews and the Sabaeans
        and the Christians, Magians and idolators,
Allah will distinguish between them on the Day of Rising.
    Allah is witness of all things.

                                          (Qur'an 22: 17)

Again, when addressing the Muslims, God says:

You are the best nation ever to be produced before mankind.
    You enjoin the right,
        forbid the wrong
            and believe in Allah.
    If the People of the Book were to believe,
        it would be better for them.
    Some of them are believers
        but most of them are deviators.

They will not harm you
    except with abusive words.
If they fight you,
    they will turn their backs on you.
Then they will not be helped.

They will be plunged into abasement
    wherever they are found,

unless they have a treaty with Allah
    and with the people.
They have brought down anger from Allah upon themselves,
    and they have been plunged into destitution.
That was because they rejected Allah's Signs
    and killed the Prophets without any right to do so.
That was because they disobeyed
    and went beyond the limits.

They are not all the same.
There is a community among the People of the Book
    who are upright.
They recite Allah's Signs throughout the night,
    and they prostrate.

They believe in Allah and the Last Day,
    and enjoin the right
        and forbid the wrong,
            and compete in doing good.
    They are among the righteous.

You will not be denied the reward
    for any good thing you do.
Allah knows those who are godfearing.   (*Qur'an* 3: 110-115)

And:

Among the People of the Book
    there are some who believe in Allah
and in what has been sent down to you
    and what was sent down to them,
        and who are humble before Allah.
    They do not sell Allah's Signs for a paltry price.
Such people will have their reward with their Lord.
    And Allah is swift at reckoning.

(*Qur'an* 3: 199)

And:

Those We gave the Book before this believe in it.
    When it is recited to them they say,
'We believe in it; it is the truth from our Lord.
    We were already Muslims before it came.'

They will be given their reward twice over
    because they have been steadfast
and because they ward off the bad with the good
    and give from what We have provided for them.

When they hear worthless talk they turn away from it
    and say, 'We have our actions and you have your actions.
        Peace be upon you.
    We do not desire the company of the ignorant.'

                                      (Qur'an 28: 52-55*)*

And:

You who believe! have taqwa of Allah
    and believe in His Messenger.
He will give you a double portion of His mercy
    and grant you a Light by which to walk
        and forgive you.
Allah is Ever-Forgiving, Most Merciful.

So that the People of the Book may know
    that they have no power at all
        over any of Allah's favour
and that all favour is in the Hand of Allah.
    He gives it to anyone He wills.
Allah's favour is indeed immense.   *(Qur'an* 57: 28-29*)*

And:

Only argue with the People of the Book in the kindest way –
    except in the case of those of them who do wrong –
saying, 'We believe in what has been sent down to us
    and what was sent down to you.
Our God and your God are One and we submit to Him.'

                                        (Qur'an 29: 46*)*

It is clear from the following passages, however, that not all of the
Jews and the Christians have the same attitude or degree of understanding:

They say, 'No one will enter the Garden
    except for Jews and Christians.'
Such is their vain hope.

Say: 'Produce your evidence if you are telling the truth.'

Not so! All who submit themselves completely to Allah
and are good-doers
will find their reward with their Lord.
They will feel no fear and will know no sorrow.

The Jews say,
'The Christians have nothing to stand on,'
and the Christians say,
'The Jews have nothing to stand on,'
yet they both recite the Book.
Those who do not know say the same as they say.
Allah will judge between them on the Day of Rising
regarding the things about which they differ.

(Qur'an 2: 111-113)

And:

The Jews and Christians say, 'We are Allah's children
and His loved ones.'
Say: 'Why, then, does He punish you for your wrong actions?
No, you are merely human beings
among those He has created.
He forgives whomever He wills
and He punishes whomever He wills.
The kingdom of the heavens and the earth
and everything between them
belongs to Allah.
He is our final destination.   *(Qur'an* 5: 18)

And certainly God makes it clear that He can forgive anything except *shirk*, which is worshipping other than Him instead of Him:

Allah does not forgive anything being associated with Him
but He forgives whomever He wills
for anything other than that.
Anyone who associates something with Allah
has gone very far astray.

(Qur'an 4: 116)

And certainly God makes it clear that it is He Who decides who is
for the Fire and who is for the Garden, and not anyone else:

> But as for those who believe and do right actions,
>   We will admit them into Gardens
>   with rivers flowing under them,
> remaining in them timelessly, for ever and ever.
>   Allah's promise is true.
> Whose speech could be truer than Allah's?

> It is not a matter of wishful thinking on your part
>   nor of the wishful thinking of the People of the Book.
>   Anyone who does evil will be repaid for it.
> He will not find any protector or helper besides Allah.

> Anyone, male or female, who does right actions
>   and is a believer,
>   will enter the Garden.
> They will not be wronged by so much as the tiniest speck.

> Who could have a better deen than someone
>   who submits himself completely to Allah
>   and is a good-doer,
> and follows the religion of Ibrahim,
>   a man of pure natural belief?
> Allah took Ibrahim as an intimate friend.

> What is in the heavens and in the earth belongs to Allah.
>   Allah encompasses all things.
>
> *(Qur'an* 4: 122-126)

Thus it is the pure and simple life-transaction embodied by Abraham to which all believers today are called :

> They say, 'Be Jews or Christians and you will be guided.'
>   Say, 'Rather adopt the religion of Ibrahim,
>   a man of natural pure belief.
> He was not one of the idolators.'

> Say: 'We believe in Allah
>   and what has been sent down to us
> and what was sent down to Ibrahim

and Isma'il and Ishaq
and Ya'qub and the Tribes,
and what Musa and 'Isa were given,
and what all the Prophets were given by their Lord.
We do not differentiate between any of them.
We are Muslims submitted to Him.'

If their faith is the same as yours
then they are guided.
But if they turn away,
they are entrenched in hostility.
Allah will be enough for you against them.
He is the All-Hearing, the All-Knowing.

The colouring of Allah –
and what colouring could be better than Allah's?
It is Him we worship.'

Say: 'Do you argue with us about Allah
when He is our Lord and your Lord?
We have our actions and you have your actions.
We act for Him alone.'
Or do they say that Ibrahim and Isma'il and Ishaq
and Ya'qub and the Tribes were Jews or Christians?
Say: 'Do you know better or does Allah?'

(*Qur'an* 2: 135-140)

Thus the *Qur'an* makes it clear that the Muslims are those who believe not only in the Prophet Muhammad, may God bless him and grant him peace, but also in all the Prophets who came before him, may the blessings and peace of God be on all of them – and in the One Who sent them, and in the prophetic life-transaction which they all shared and embodied:

Say, 'People of the Book! come to a proposition
which is the same for us and you –
that we should worship none but Allah
and not associate any partners with Him
and not take one another as lords besides Allah.'
If they turn away, say, 'Bear witness that we are Muslims.'

People of the Book! why do you argue concerning Ibrahim
    when the *Torah* and *Injil* were only sent down after him?
      Why do you not use your intellect?
You are people arguing about something
    of which you have no knowledge.
Why do you argue about something
    of which you have no knowledge?
      Allah knows; you do not know.'

Ibrahim was neither a Jew nor a Christian,
    but a man of pure natural belief – a Muslim.
He was not one of the idolators.

The people with the strongest claim to Ibrahim
    are those who followed him
      and this Prophet (Muhammad)
    and those who believe.
Allah is the Protector of the believers.

A group of the People of the Book
    would love to misguide you.
They only misguide themselves
    but they are not aware of it.

People of the Book! why do you reject Allah's Signs
    when you yourselves are there as witnesses?

People of the Book! why do you mix truth with falsehood
    and knowingly conceal the truth?

A group of the People of the Book say,
    'At the beginning of the day,
      you should claim to believe
in what was sent down to those who believe,
    and then at the end of the day, you should reject it,
      so that hopefully they will revert.
Do not trust anyone except for those
    who follow your own deen.'
Say: 'Allah's guidance is true guidance.
    But you think it is impossible for anyone
to be given the same as you were given,
    or to argue with you before your Lord.'

Say, 'All favour is in Allah's hand
and He gives it to whomever He wills.
Allah is All-Encompassing, All-Knowing.
He picks out for His mercy whomever He wills.
Allah's favour is indeed immense.'

Among the People of the Book there are some who,
if you entrust them with a pile of gold,
will return it to you.
But there are others among them who,
if you entrust them with just a single dinar,
will not return it to you,
unless you stay standing over them.
That is because they say,
'We are under no obligation
where the gentiles are concerned.'
They tell a lie against Allah and they know it.

No, the truth is, if people honour their contracts
and have taqwa of Him,
Allah loves those who are godfearing.

Those who sell Allah's contract and their own oaths
for a paltry price,
such people will have no portion in the Next World
and on the Day of Rising Allah will not speak to them
or look at them
or purify them.
They will have a painful punishment.

Among them is a group who distort the Book
with their tongues
so that you think it is from the Book
when it is not from the Book.
They say, 'It is from Allah,' but it is not from Allah.
They tell a lie against Allah and they know it.

It is not right for any human being
that Allah should give him the Book
and Judgement and Prophethood,

and then that he should say to people,
  'Be worshippers of me rather than Allah.'
Rather he will say, 'Be people of the Lord
    because of your knowledge of the Book
      and because you study.'

He would never command you to take
    the angels and Prophets as Lords.
Would he command you to disbelieve
    after being Muslim?

Remember when Allah made a covenant with the Prophets:
  'Now that We have given you a share
      of the Book and Wisdom,
    and then a Messenger comes to you
        confirming what is with you,
    you must believe in him and help him.'
He asked, 'Do you agree and undertake My commission
    on that condition?'
They replied, 'We agree.'
    He said, 'Bear witness, then.
I am with you as one of the witnesses.'

Any who turn away after that
    are deviators.

Is it other than the deen of Allah that you desire,
    when everything in the heavens and earth,
        willingly or unwillingly,
          submits to Him
    and to Him you will be returned?

Say: 'We believe in Allah
    and what has been sent down to us
and what was sent down to Ibrahim, Isma'il and Ishaq
    and Ya'qub and the Tribes,
and what Musa and 'Isa and all the Prophets
    were given by their Lord.
We do not differentiate between any of them.
    We are Muslims submitted to Him.'

> If anyone desires anything other than Islam as a deen,
> > it will not be accepted from him,
> and in the Next World he will be among the losers.
>
> > > > *(Qur'an 3: 64-85)*

The *Qur'an* also confirms that even though some of the People of the Book know that their teachings have been altered and that the teachings of the Prophet Muhammad are pure, they still nevertheless prefer the falsehood to the truth:

> Allah made a covenant with those given the Book:
> > 'You must make it clear to people and not conceal it.'
> But they toss it in disdain behind their backs
> > and sell it for a paltry price.
> What an evil sale they make!
>
> Those who exult in what they have done
> > and love to be praised for what they have not done
> should not suppose that they have escaped the punishment.
> > They will have a painful punishment.
>
> The kingdom of the heavens and earth belongs to Allah.
> > Allah has power over all things.
> > > > *(Qur'an 3: 187-189)*

And:

> Do you not see those who were given a portion of the Book
> > trading in misguidance
> and wanting you to be misguided from the way?
> > Allah knows best who your enemies are.
> Allah suffices as a Protector; Allah suffices as a Helper.
> > > > *(Qur'an 4: 44)*

And:

> Those We have given the Book recognise it
> > as they recognise their own children.
> As for those who have lost their own selves,
> > they do not believe.   *(Qur'an 6: 20)*

And:

> Say: 'People of the Book, why do you reject Allah's Signs
> > when Allah is witness of everything you do?'

Say: 'People of the Book, why do you bar
　　those who believe from the Way of Allah,
　　　　desiring to make it crooked,
　　when you yourselves are witnesses to it?
Allah is not unaware of what you do.'

You who believe!
　　if you obey a group of those given the Book,
　　　　they will make you revert to being unbelievers
　　after you have have believed.

How can you disbelieve, when Allah's Signs are recited to you
　　and the Messenger is there among you?
Whoever holds fast to Allah
　　has been guided to a straight path.

You who believe! have taqwa of Allah
　　with the taqwa due to Him
and do not die except as Muslims.　　　(*Qur'an* 3: 98-102)

God tells the followers of the Prophet Muhammad what to say to
those of the People of the Book who oppose the Muslims:

Say: 'People of the Book! do you resent us
　　for any other reason
　　　　than that we believe in Allah
　　and what was sent down to us,
　　　　and what was sent down before,
　　and because most of you are deviators?'

Say: 'Shall I tell you of a reward with Allah
　　far worse than that:
　　　　that of those whom Allah has cursed
　　　　　　and with whom He is angry –
　　turning some of them into monkeys and into pigs –
　　　　and who worshipped false gods?
　　Such people are in a worse situation
　　　　and further from the right way.'

When they come to you, they say, 'We believe.'
　　But they entered with unbelief and left with it.
Allah knows best what they were hiding.

You see many of them rushing to wrongdoing and enmity
and acquiring ill-gotten gains.
What an evil thing they do!

Why do their scholars and rabbis not prohibit them
from evil speech and acquiring ill-gotten gains?
What an evil thing they invent!

(*Qur'an* 5: 59-63)

And:

The Jews say, "Uzayr is the son of Allah,'
and the Christians say, 'The Messiah is the son of Allah.'
That is what they say with their mouths,
copying the words of those who disbelieved before.
Allah fight them! How perverted they are!

They have taken their rabbis and monks
as lords besides Allah,
and also the Messiah, son of Maryam.
Yet they were commanded to worship only one God.
There is no god but Him!
Glory be to Him above anything they associate with Him!

They desire to extinguish Allah's Light with their mouths.
But Allah refuses to do other than perfect His Light,
even though the unbelievers detest it.

It is He who sent His Messenger
with guidance and the Deen of Truth
to exalt it over every other deen,
even though the idolators detest it.

You who believe! many of the rabbis and monks
devour people's property under false pretences
and bar people from access to the Way of Allah.
As for those who hoard up gold and silver
and do not spend it in the Way of Allah,
give them the news of a painful punishment
on the Day it is heated up in the fire of Hell
and their foreheads, sides and backs are branded with it:
'This is what you hoarded for yourselves,
so taste what you were hoarding!' (*Qur'an* 9: 30-35)

Fortunately not all of the People of the Book oppose the Muslims with the same degree of intensity:

> You will find that the people most hostile
>   to those who believe
>   are the Jews and the idolators.
> You will find the people most affectionate
>   to those who believe
>   are those who say, 'We are Christians.'
> That is because some of them are priests and monks
>   and because they are not arrogant.
>
> When they listen to what has been sent down
>   to the Messenger,
>   you see their eyes overflowing with tears
>   because of what they recognise of the truth.
> They say, 'Our Lord, we believe!
>   So write us down among the witnesses.
> How could we not believe in Allah,
>   and the truth that has come to us, when
> we long for our Lord to include us among the righteous?'
>
> Allah will reward them for what they say
>   with Gardens with rivers flowing under them,
>   remaining in them timelessly, for ever.
>   That is the recompense of the good-doers.
>
> As for those who disbelieve and deny Our Signs,
>   they are the Companions of the Blazing Fire.
>
> (Qur'an 5: 82-86)

It is clear from the *Qur'an*, however, that wherever their sympathies may lie, those Christians who refuse to accept Islam are more closely allied with the Jews than with the Muslims, and God warns the Muslims not to take them as their friends:

> The Jews and the Christians will never be pleased with you
>   until you follow their religion.
> Say: 'Allah's guidance is the true guidance.'
>   If you were to follow their whims and desires,
>   after the knowledge that has come to you,
> you would find no protector or helper against Allah.

Those to whom We have given the Book,
  who recite it in the way it should be recited,
    such people believe in it.
As for those who reject it, they are the losers.

(*Qur'an* 2: 120-121)

And:

You who believe! do not take the Jews and Christians
    as your friends;
  they are the friends of one another.
Any of you who takes them as friends is one of them.
  Allah does not guide wrongdoing people.

Yet you see those with sickness in their hearts
    rushing to them,
  saying, 'We fear the wheel of fate may turn against us.'
But it may well be that Allah will bring about victory
  or some other contingency from Him.
Then they will deeply regret their secret thoughts.

Those who believe say,
  'Are these the people who swore by Allah,
    with their most earnest oaths,
      that they were with you?'
Their actions have come to nothing and they now are losers.

(*Qur'an* 5: 51-53)

And:

You who believe! do not take as friends
  any of those given the Book before you or the unbelievers
    who make a mockery and a game out of your deen.
  Have taqwa of Allah if you are believers.

When you call to the prayer,
  they make a mockery and a game of it.
That is because they are a people
  who do not use their intellect.   (*Qur'an* 5: 57-58)

And:

You who believe! do not take
  any outside yourselves as intimates.

They will do anything to harm you.
 They love what causes you distress.
Hatred has appeared out of their mouths,
 but what their breasts hide is far worse.
We have made the Signs clear to you
 if you use your intellect.

There you are, loving them when they do not love you,
 even though you believe in all the Books.
When they meet you, they say, 'We believe.'
 But when they leave they bite their fingers
  out of rage against you.
 Say: 'Die in your rage.'
Allah knows what your hearts contain.

If something good happens to you, it galls them.
 If something bad strikes you, they rejoice at it.
But if you are steadfast and are godfearing,
 their scheming will not harm you in any way.
Allah encompasses what they do.

(*Qur'an* 3: 118-120)

God tells the followers of the Prophet Muhammad how to treat those from among the People of the Book who are openly opposed to the Muslims:

Fight those of the people who were given the Book
 who do not believe in Allah and the Last Day
  and who do not make unlawful
 what Allah and His Messenger have made unlawful
  and do not take as their deen the deen of Truth,
until they pay the jizya with their own hands
 in a state of complete abasement.   (*Qur'an* 9: 29)

In spite of sustained opposition throughout the last fourteen centuries to God, and to the Prophet Muhammad, may God bless him and grant him peace, and to the *Qur'an*, the invitation to the People of the Book in every age to obey God and His Messenger has always remained the same:

People of the Book! Our Messenger has come to you,

> making clear to you much of the Book
>   that you have kept concealed,
>   and passing over a lot.
> A Light has come to you from Allah
>   and a Clear Book.
>
> By it, Allah guides
>   those who follow what pleases Him
>   to the ways of Peace.
> He will bring them from the darkness to the light
>   by His permission,
> and guide them to a straight path.   (*Qur'an* 5: 15-16)

And:

> People of the Book! Our Messenger has come to you,
>   making things clear to you,
>   after a period with no Messengers,
>   lest you should say,
>   'No one came to us bringing good news or warning.'
> Someone has come to you
>   bringing good news and a warning.
> Allah has power over all things.   (*Qur'an* 5: 19)

God also says in the *Qur'an*:

> In the name of Allah, All-Merciful, Most Merciful
>
> The People of the Book who disbelieved and the idolators
>   would not be cut off until the Clear Sign came to them:
> a Messenger from Allah reciting purified texts
>   containing upright precepts.
>
> Those who were given the Book did not divide into sects
>   until after the Clear Sign came to them.
> They were only ordered to worship Allah,
>   making their deen sincerely His
>   as people of pure natural faith,
> and to establish the prayer and pay zakat –
>   that is the correct deen.
>
> The People of the Book who disbelieve and the idolators

will be in the Fire of Hell,
    remaining in it timelessly, for ever.
They are the worst of creatures.
But those who believe and do right actions –
    they are the best of creatures.
Their reward is with their Lord:
    Gardens of Eden with rivers flowing under them,
        remaining in them timelessly, for ever and ever.
    Allah is pleased with them
        and they are pleased with Him.
This is for those who fear their Lord.   (*Qur'an* 98: 1-8)

And:

He who has purified himself will have success,
    he who invokes the Name of his Lord and prays.
Yet still you prefer the life of this world
    when the Next World is better and longer lasting.

This is certainly in the earlier texts,
    the texts of Ibrahim and Musa.   (*Qur'an* 87: 14-19)

Again, in *Surat al-Mai'da*, God reminds the People of the Book of
the reward that awaits those who follow the Prophet Muhammad –
the same reward which awaits whoever has truly followed not only
Moses and Jesus, but indeed all of the Prophets and Messengers
who came before and after them, may the blessings and peace of
God be on all of them:

If only the People of the Book had believed
    and been godfearing,
    We would have erased their evil deeds from them
        and admitted them into Gardens of Delight.

If only they had implemented the *Torah* and the *Injil*
    and what was sent down to them from their Lord,
they would have been fed from above their heads
    and beneath their feet.
Among them there is a moderate group
    but what most of them do is evil.   (*Qur'an* 5: 65-66)

And:

Say: 'People of the Book! you have nothing to stand on
　　until you implement the *Torah* and the *Injil*
and what has been sent down to you from your Lord.'
　　What has been sent down to you from your Lord
　　　　increases many of them in insolence and unbelief.
So do not waste your grief on the people of the unbelievers.

(Qur'an 5: 68)

And:

Say: 'People of the Book! do not go to extremes in your deen,
　　asserting other than the truth,
and do not follow the whims and desires of people
　　who were misguided previously
and have misguided many others,
　　and are far from the right way.'　　*(Qur'an 5: 77)*

When describing those who believe in the signs of God – including
the Prophet Muhammad, may God bless him and grant him peace
– God refers to:

those who follow the Messenger,
　　the Unlettered Prophet,
whom they find written down with them
　　in the *Torah* and the *Injil,*
commanding them to do right
　　and forbidding them to do wrong,
making good things lawful for them
　　and bad things unlawful for them,
relieving them of their heavy loads
　　and the chains which were around them.
Those who believe in him
　　and honour him and help him,
and follow the Light that has been sent down with him,
　　they are the ones who are successful.

Say (O Muhammad): 'Mankind! I am the Messenger of Allah
　　to you all,
of Him to whom the kingdom of the heavens
　　and the earth belongs.
There is no god but Him.

He gives life and causes to die.'
So believe in Allah and His Messenger,
   the Unlettered Prophet,
who believes in Allah and His words,
   and follow him
so that hopefully you will be guided.   (*Qur'an* 7: 157-158)

And:

You have an excellent model in the Messenger of Allah,
   for all who put their hope in Allah and the Last Day
      and remember Allah much.

(*Qur'an* 33: 21)

And:

Muhammad is not the father of any of your men,
   but the Messenger of Allah
      and the Final Seal of the Prophets.
   Allah has knowledge of all things.

You who believe! remember Allah much,
   and glorify Him in the morning and the evening.
It is He who calls down blessing on you,
   as do His angels,
to bring you out of the darkness into the light.
   He is Most Merciful to the believers.
Their greeting on the Day they meet Him will be 'Peace!'
   and He has prepared a generous reward for them.

(*Qur'an* 33: 40-44)

And:

You who believe! bow and prostrate
      and worship your Lord,
   and do good, so that hopefully you will be successful.
Do jihad for Allah with the jihad due to Him.
   He has selected you and not placed
      any constraint upon you in the deen –
   the religion of your forefather Ibrahim.
He named you Muslims before and also in this,
   so that the Messenger could be witness against you
      and you could be witnesses against all mankind.

So establish the prayer and pay zakat
and hold fast to Allah.
He is your Protector –
the Best Protector, the Best Helper.   (*Qur'an* 22: 77-78)

And:

Whoever obeys Allah and the Messenger
will be with those whom Allah has blessed:
the Prophets and the truly sincere,
the martyrs, and the righteous.
What excellent company such people are!   (*Qur'an* 4: 69)

And:

He has laid down the same deen for you
as He enjoined on Nuh:
that which We have revealed to you
and which We enjoined on Ibrahim, Musa and 'Isa:
'Establish the deen and do not make divisions in it.'
What you call the idolators to follow is very hard for them.
Allah chooses for Himself anyone He wills
and guides to Himself those who turn to Him.

They only split up after knowledge came to them,
tyrannising one another.
And were it not for a prior decree from your Lord
for a specified term,
the judgement between them
would already have been made.
Those who inherited the Book after them
are indeed in grave doubt about it.
(*Qur'an* 42: 13-14)

And:

The deen in the sight of Allah is Islam.
Those given the Book only differed
after knowledge had come to them,
envying one another.
As for those who reject Allah's Signs,
Allah is swift at reckoning.

If they argue with you, say,

'I have submitted myself completely to Allah,
    and so have all who follow me.'
Say to those given the Book and those who have no Book,
    'Have you become Muslim?'
If they become Muslim, they have been guided.
If they turn away, you are only responsible for transmission.
    Allah sees His slaves.

As for those who reject Allah's Signs,
    and kill the Prophets without any right to do so,
      and kill those who command justice,
    give them news of a painful punishment.

They are the ones whose actions come to nothing
    in this world or the Next World.
They will have no helpers.

Do you not see those who have been given
      a portion of the Book
    being invited to let Allah's Book
      be the judge between them?
    But then a group of them turn away.

That is because they say,
    'The Fire will only touch us for a number of days.'
Their inventions have deluded them in their deen.

But how will it be when We gather them all together
    for a Day about which there is no doubt?
Every self will be paid in full for what it earned.
    They will not be wronged.

                          (*Qur'an* 3: 19-25)

And:

The parties differed among themselves.
    Woe to those who disbelieve
when they are present on a terrible Day!

How clear will be their hearing,
    how perfect their sight,
      on the Day they come to Us;
    whereas today the wrongdoers
      are clearly misguided.

Warn them of the Day of Bitter Regret
    when the affair will be resolved.
But they take no notice.
    They do not believe.

It is We who will inherit the earth
    and all those on it.
They will be returned to Us.   (*Qur'an* 19: 37-40)

And:

What will convey to you what the Day of Judgement is?
    Again, what will convey to you
        what the Day of Judgement is?
It is the Day when a self will have no power
    to help any other self in any way.
The command that Day will be Allah's alone.
                        (*Qur'an* 82: 17-19)

And:

Say, 'O Allah! Master of the Kingdom!
    You give sovereignty to whomever You will
    You take sovereignty from whomever You will.
    You exalt whomever You will
    You abase whomever You will.
        All good is in Your hands.
    You have power over all things.
    You merge the night into the day.
    You merge the day into the night.
    You bring out the living from the dead.
    You bring out the dead from the living.
    You provide for whomever You will
        without any reckoning.   (*Qur'an* 3: 26-27)

And:

In the name of Allah, All-Merciful, Most Merciful

Say: 'He is Allah, Absolute Oneness,
Allah, the Everlasting Sustainer of all.
He has not given birth and was not born.
And no one is comparable to Him.'   (*Qur'an* 112: 1-4)

And:

In the name of Allah, All-Merciful, Most Merciful

Praise be to Allah, the Lord of all the worlds,
the All-Merciful, the Most Merciful,
the King of the Day of Judgment.

You alone we worship.
You alone we ask for help.

Guide us on the Straight Path,
the Path of those You have blessed,
not of those with anger on them,
nor of the misguided.

(*Qur'an* 1: 1-7)

Amin

✿   ✿   ✿   ✿   ✿

And when Allah says, "Isa son of Maryam! Did you say to people, "Take me and my mother as gods besides Allah?"' he will say, 'Glory be to You! It is not for me to say what I have no right to say! If I had said it, then You would have known it. You know what is in my self but I do not know what is in Your Self. You are the Knower of all unseen things. I said to them nothing but what You ordered me to say: "Worship Allah, my Lord and your Lord." I was a witness against them as long as I remained among them, but when You took me back to You, You were the One watching over them. You are Witness of all things.

(Qur'an: Surat al-Ma'ida – 5: 116-117)

Glossary

Allah : God, may He be exalted and glorified.

Ahmad : another name of the Prophet Muhammad, may Allah bless him and grant him peace.

akhira : the Next World, what is on the other side of death.

ayat : lit. sign, a verse of the *Qur'an*.

Ayyub : the Prophet Job, peace be upon him.

Dawud : the Prophet David, peace be upon him.

deen : life-transaction, religion in the broadest sense. The deen of Allah and the Muslim community is Islam but every society and cultural grouping have a deen which they follow.

Dhu'n-Nun : 'He of the Whale', another name for the Prophet Yunus, peace be upon him.

dinar : a pure gold coin 4.25 grams in weight.

dirham : a pure silver coin 3.00 grams in weight.

dunya : this world, not as cosmic phenomenon, but as experienced.

Furqan : something which discriminates between truth and falsehood; another name for the Qur'an.

halal : lawful in the Shari'a.

haram : unlawful in the Shari'a.

Harun : the Prophet Aaron, peace be upon him.

Iblis : the personal name of the Devil, lit. 'seized by despair'. He is also called Shaytan or the 'enemy of Allah'.

Ibrahim : the Prophet Abraham, peace be upon him.

Ilyas :	also Ilyasin, the Prophet Elijah or Elias, peace be upon him.
iman :	belief, faith, acceptance in the heart of Allah and His Messenger. Iman consists of believing in Allah, His angels, His Books, His Messengers, the Last Day, the Garden and the Fire, and that everything, both good and bad, is by the decree of Allah.
'Imran :	the Biblical Amran, the father of Musa and Harun. Also the name of Maryam's father.
Injil :	the Gospel, the revelation given to the Prophet 'Isa.
'Isa :	the Prophet Jesus, peace be upon him.
Ishaq :	the Prophet Isaac, peace be upon him.
Isma'il :	the Prophet Ishmael, peace be upon him.
Isra'il :	Israel, the Prophet Ya'qub or Jacob, peace be upon him.
Jibril :	or Jibra'il, the angel Gabriel, who informed Maryam of the birth of 'Isa, who brought the revelation of the *Injil* to the Prophet 'Isa and who brought the revelation of the *Qur'an* to the Prophet Muhammad, may Allah bless him and grant him peace.
jihad :	struggle, particularly fighting in the way of Allah to establish Islam.
jinn :	inhabitants of the heavens and the earth made of smokeless fire who are usually invisible.
jizya :	an annual protection tax payable by adult male non-Muslims as a tribute to a Muslim ruler, traditionally 4 dinars or 40 dirhams.
kafir :	someone who rejects Allah and His Messenger and the deen of Islam.

kafirun :   the plural of kafir.

kuffar :   the plural of kafir.

kufr :   disbelief, to cover up the truth, to reject Allah and refuse to believe that Muhammad is His Messenger.

Lut :   the Prophet Lot, peace be upon him.

Maryam :   Mary, the mother of 'Isa, peace be upon her.

Muhammad :   the Prophet Muhammad, may Allah bless him and grant him peace, the last of the Messengers sent by God to mankind and the jinn.

mumin :   someone who possesses iman.

muminun :   the plural of mumin.

munafiq :   a hypocrite, someone who outwardly professes Islam on the tongue, but inwardly rejects Allah and His Messenger.

munafiqun :   the plural of munafiq.

Musa :   the Prophet Moses, peace be upon him.

mushrik :   someone who commits the unforgivable wrong action of worshipping something or someone other than Allah or of ascribing to something or someone attributes which in fact belong to Allah alone.

mushrikun :   the plural of mushrik.

Nuh :   the Prophet Noah, peace be upon him.

Qur'an :   'the Recitation', the uncreated word of Allah, the last revelation from God to mankind and the jinn, revealed to the Prophet Muhammad, which confirms, amends, encompasses, expands and abrogates all the earlier revelations sent down to the earlier messengers, blessings and peace be upon all of them.

riba :	usury, which is forbidden, whatever forms it takes, since it involves obtaining something for nothing through exploitation.
Ruh :	the soul, vital spirit, the breath of life which emanates from Allah to His creatures. Purest Ruh is a name given to the angel Jibril.
sadaqa :	voluntary charitable giving for the sake of Allah.
sadiqun :	truthful, true, sincere people, a term given to a high category of the muminun.
salat :	the prayer, particularly the five daily obligatory prayers which constitute one of the pillars of Islam.
salih :	someone who acts rightly.
salihun :	the plural of salih.
shaytan :	a devil, particularly Iblis, one of the jinn.
Shari'a :	lit. road, the legal modality of a people based on the Revelation of their Prophet. The final Shari'a is that of Islam.
shirk :	the unforgiveable wrong action of worshipping something or someone other than Allah or associating something or someone as a partner with Him.
siddiq :	someone who is true to their word and absolutely sincere and unshakeable in their iman.
siddiqun :	the plural of siddiq.
sidq :	truthfulness, sincerity, the quality possessed by the siddiq.
Sulayman :	the Prophet Solomon, peace be upon him.
sura :	lit. form, a chapter of the *Qur'an*.

taqwa : awe or fear of Allah, which inspires a person to be on guard against wrong action and eager for actions which please Him.

Torah : the revelation given to the Prophet Musa.

the Tribes : the Tribes of Israel, descended from the twelve sons of the Prophet Ya'qub or Jacob.

'Uzayr : the Prophet Ezra, peace be upon him.

Yahya : the Prophet John the Baptist, peace be upon him, the son of Zakariyya.

Ya'qub : the Prophet Jacob, peace be upon him, also called Isra'il.

al-Yasa' : the Prophet Elisha, peace be upon him.

Yunus : the Prophet Jonah, peace be upon him.

Yusha' : Joshua.

Yusuf : the Prophet Joseph, peace be upon him.

Zabur : the Psalms, the revelation given to the Prophet Dawud.

Zakariyya : the Prophet Zachariah, peace be upon him, the father of Yahya and the guardian of Maryam.

zakat : one of the five pillars of Islam. It is an obligatory wealth tax paid on certain forms of wealth: gold and silver, staple crops, livestock, and trading goods, when they are over a certain amount.

❂   ❂   ❂   ❂   ❂